5/10

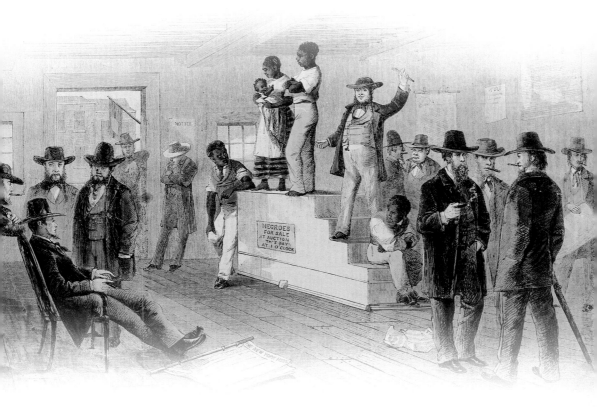

Documenting History

Documenting Slavery and Civil Rights

Philip Steele

rosen publishing's
rosen central
New York

Published in 2010 by The Rosen Publishing Group Inc.
29 East 21st Street, New York, NY 10010

First Edition

Senior editor: Camilla Lloyd
Designer: Phipps Design
Consultant: Dr. John Stuart
Picture researcher: Shelley Noronha
Indexer and proofreader: Cath Senker
Map: Ian Thompson

Library of Congress Cataloging-in-Publication Data

Steele, Philip, 1948-
 Documenting slavery and civil rights / Philip Steele.
     p. cm. -- (Documenting history)
 Includes index.
 ISBN 978-1-4358-9671-0 (library binding)
 ISBN 978-1-4358-9676-5 (paperback)
 ISBN 978-1-4358-9679-6 (6-pack)
 1. Slavery--History--Sources--Juvenile literature. 2. Slavery--United States--History--
 Sources--Juvenile literature. 3. Antislavery movements--United States--History--19th
 century--Sources--Juvenile literature. 4. African Americans--Civil rights--Southern
 States--
 History--Sources--Juvenile literature. I. Title.
 HT863.S697 2010
 306.3'62--dc22
                          2009025863

Photo Credits:
The author and publisher would like to thank the following for allowing their pictures to
be reproduced in this publication: Cover: Main: Bettmann/Corbis , BL: Topfoto, Background:
Wayland Picture Library ; 1 Wayland Picture Library, 4 Bibliotheque Nationale, Paris,
France,/The Bridgeman Art Library, 5 Topham Picturepoint, 6 Werner Forman Archive/
British Museum, London. Location: 09, 7 Werner Forman Archive, 9 Peter Newark
American Pictures /The Bridgeman Art Library, 11 Wayland Piccture Library, 12 Photo ©
Christie's Images /The Bridgeman Art Library, 13, 14 Wayland Picture Library, 15 Royal
Albert Memorial Museum, Exeter, Devon, U.K./The Bridgeman Art Library, 16 Bibliotheque
des Arts Decoratifs, Paris, France, Archives Charmet /The Bridgeman Art Library, 17
Bibliotheque Nationale, Paris, France, Archives Charmet /The Bridgeman Art Library, 18 ©
Wilberforce House, Hull City Museums and Art Galleries, U.K.,/The Bridgeman Art Library,
19 Bettmann/CORBIS, 20 © Royal Geographical Society, London, U.K.,/The Bridgeman Art
Library, 21 Library of Congress, 22 National Library of Australia, 23 Private Collection, ©
Michael Graham-Stewart / The Bridgeman Art Library, 24 Everett Collection/Rex
Features, 25 Topfoto, 26 Wayland Picture Library, 27 Library of Congress, 28
Bettmann/CORBIS, 29 © Collection of the New-York Historical Society, U.S.A.,/The
Bridgeman Art Library, 30 c. Wisc Hist/Everett/Rex Features, 31 Peter Newark American
Pictures /The Bridgeman Art Library, 32 Time & Life Pictures/Getty, 33 Bettmann/Corbis,
34 Topfoto, 37 Everett Collection/Rex Features, 38 Topham Picturepoint, 41 Everett
Collection/Rex Features, 42 Michael Ainsworth/Dallas Morning News/Corbis, 43 Kristin
Callahan/Rex Features, 44 Wang Ying/Xinhua Press/Corbis

Acknowledgments: 21 Naval Orders found in The Royal Naval Museum.

Manufactured in China
CPSIA Compliance Information: Batch #WAW0102YA: For Further Information
contact Rosen Publishing, New York, New York at 1-800-237-9932

CONTENTS

Origins of slavery

A slave is someone who is deprived of his or her freedom and forced to work for other people without reward. Slaves are treated as the property of the slave owner and may be bought or sold.

This painting from 1237 shows African slaves being sold at an Arab market. It is an illustration from a version of the **Maqamat,** *a collection of tales written in about 1100 by al-Hariri of Basrah. Slavery has existed throughout history and caused untold misery around the world.*

Slavery is one example of unfree labor or servitude. Other examples include debt bondage, in which someone who cannot repay a debt is forced to work for no reward as compensation for the debt. Indenture is a contract for a limited term, during which the worker gives up the right to

withdraw labor or move away. Child labor is the employment of children for low or no wages, often without rights or the protection of the law. Sexual slavery is enforced prostitution.

Slavery and some other forms of servitude are as old as human history. Warriors or civilians captured in wars were often taken as slaves, and convicted criminals could also be sentenced to slavery. Refugees from warfare, victims of natural disasters, children, and others unable to defend themselves were at risk from raiders, who might capture them to sell as slaves. The children of slaves

WRITING

"No master can feel safe because he is kind and considerate; for it is [the slaves'] brutality, not their reasoning capacity, which leads [them] to murder their masters."

Brutality is blamed on the slaves themselves rather than on the owners who treat them brutally.

Pliny the Younger (ca. 61–113 CE), Roman lawyer and writer.

would often be born into slavery, forming a subclass of society with no rights as citizens.

Peoples in almost every part of the world have at some point in their history been slave owners or slaves. Slavery was common in the earliest civilizations, being the practice in Mesopotamia (modern Iraq) as early as 3500 BCE. Chinese rulers and nobles owned slaves more than 3,000 years ago. When a ruler died, his slaves might be killed and buried with him, to serve him in the next life.

The Ancient Greeks relied on slave labor, and although the Greeks introduced a form of democracy, or rule by citizens' assemblies, voting rights were never extended to slaves. The Romans took slaves from all over their empire, including Britons, Gauls, Germans, Dacians (inhabitants of Ancient Dacia, or present-day Romania, and parts of northern Bulgaria), Greeks, and North Africans. Slaves may have made up about one-third of Roman society. A lucky few were granted their freedom for money or as a reward for hard work, a legal process called manumission.

Some slaves were well treated in the ancient world, acting as house servants or children's tutors, but others were forced into hard labor on farms or in

SOURCE

TAG

"In the event of my running away, hold me and return me to my master Viventius on the estate of Callistus."

These were the words on a bronze tag worn around the neck of a Roman slave.

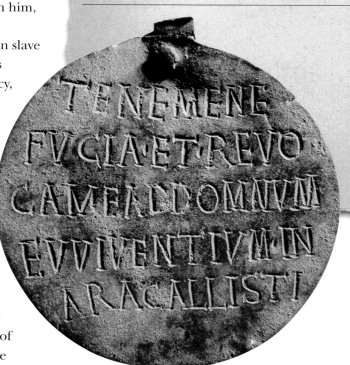

the mines. Revolts were common and one slave named Spartacus (ca. 109–71 BCE) led a huge rebel army against the government of Rome. After his defeat and death, 6,600 of his supporters were executed by crucifixion.

Africa plundered

In the European Middle Ages, the Roman pattern of slavery came to an end, although other forms of servitude, such as serfdom, were common.

Toward the end of this period, European explorers began to discover and conquer new lands in Africa, Asia, and the Americas. In 1492, the explorer Christopher Columbus, in the service of Spain, sailed across the Atlantic Ocean, beginning a period of European exploration and settlement in the Americas. These territories offered raw materials, land, and new trading opportunities. They could be developed at little expense by using slave labor.

As early as the 1440s, Portuguese seafarers were shipping African slaves back to Portugal and its overseas colonies. European colonists who settled in the Americas first enslaved Native Americans, but as the numbers of these were decimated by warfare and disease, the colonists seized Africans to take their place.

This was a religious age, but Judaism, Christianity, and Islam did not forbid slavery on moral grounds. The scriptures of all three religions included both support for slavery and either some criticism of it or at least calls for the humane treatment of slaves. Most religions permitted the enslavement of people with other religious beliefs. For centuries, Muslims along the North African ("Barbary") coast enslaved European Christians, and vice versa.

Slavery had existed in Africa long before the coming of the Europeans. As elsewhere in the world, prisoners of war, debtors, or criminals

A bronze figure from the West African empire of Benin (part of modern Nigeria) shows a Portuguese soldier with a musket. In the 1500s, the rulers of Benin traded with both the Portuguese and the English, exchanging slaves, ivory, and pepper for guns and manufactured goods.

In 1482, the Portuguese built a fort at Elmina on the coast of Ghana. It was the first European settlement in West Africa and became a center of the transatlantic slave trade for hundreds of years.

LEGAL CHARTER

"A Trade for Angola is begun, and they have Ordered a factory [trading post] to settle neer [near] the Portugal's cheife Citty [chief city] at Sunio Whence it's hoped quantities of Slaves may bee [be] got and much Copper. … The Slaves they purchas[e]d are sent for a Supply of Servants, to all His Ma[jes]tie's American Plantations which cannot subsist without them."

This is from a Royal African Company charter, listing the geographical limits of British trade in West Africa. The origins of slavery lie in economics. From 1660 to 1731, the British slave trade was entirely controlled by the Royal African Company, established by London merchants and the ruling royal family, the Stuarts.

might be enslaved. However, they were not regarded as chattels, or personal property, but rather as indentured laborers. They could often regain their freedom after a fixed term. During the Middle Ages, this African slave trade became part of an international trading network.

Slaves from sub-Saharan Africa were sold to traders and taken north across the desert. In East Africa, slaves were sold to Arab traders along the coast, and then shipped to the lands of southwest Asia. The East African slave trade predated and outlasted that of West Africa.

On the West African coast, increasing numbers of English, French, Danish, and Dutch seafarers purchased slaves and shipped them across the ocean to homes and plantations in the "New World" (as they called the Americas). It has been estimated that about 12 million Africans were uprooted from their homeland and sent to the Americas during the duration of this transatlantic slave trade.

Across the Atlantic

The shipment of slaves across the Atlantic developed into a three-way operation, the "Triangular Trade." On the outward voyage, ships from Europe brought iron, copper, textiles, beads, firearms, and liquor to West African ports. These were then traded for slaves, which were shipped to the Americas on the second leg of the voyage, the infamous Middle Passage. For the last leg of the voyage, returning to Europe, the ships took on sugar, molasses (syrup drained from raw sugar), rum, tobacco, indigo (a deep blue dye made from a shrub grown in South America and the Caribbean), cotton, and other New World exports.

The Triangular Trade between Europe, West Africa, and the New World brought slavery to a peak in the eighteenth century.

Where did the slaves come from? Since ancient times, West Africa had been ruled by a succession of powerful chiefdoms, kingdoms, and empires under which slavery was common. One ruler of Mali in the 1300s, Mansa Musa, traveled to Arabia accompanied by 12,000 personal slaves. In the 1600s and 1700s, the export of slaves, as well as the taxation of foreign traders, brought wealth to African rulers and merchants.

In West Africa, the European newcomers rarely seized the slaves for themselves. They left that to local raiders, who would attack villages and kidnap men, women, and children. All were marched to the coast, being relayed from one trader to another. The terrified survivors were then

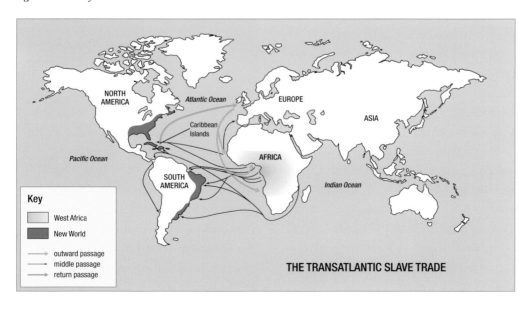

Key

- West Africa
- New World
- → outward passage
- → middle passage
- → return passage

THE TRANSATLANTIC SLAVE TRADE

locked up in pens or coastal forts, until they were sold to the Europeans.

The voyage across the Atlantic was an unimaginable horror. Millions of slaves died before ever seeing the Americas. They were often branded like cattle, fettered, and packed into the dark, stinking hold, seasick and wretched. In the eighteenth century, the voyage lasted about 12 weeks. Many caught diseases such as dysentery, scurvy, or smallpox. Those able to put up resistance to their captors were flogged, tortured, or thrown overboard. So, too, were those whose spirits sank

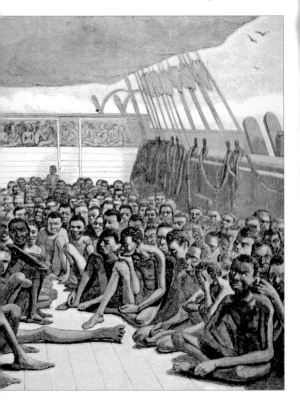

This engraving shows despairing West African slaves huddling on the deck of a European ship during the terrible ordeal of the Middle Passage.

SOURCE

BOOK

"…About eight o'clock in the morning, the Negroes are generally brought upon deck. Their irons being examined, a long chain, which is locked to a ring-bolt, fixed in the deck, is run through the rings of the shackles of the men, and then locked to another ring-bolt, fixed also in the deck. By this means fifty or sixty, and sometimes more, are fastened to one chain, in order to prevent them from rising, or endeavoring to escape …"

Alexander Falconbridge was a British surgeon who served on slave trips during the 1780s. He later campaigned against slavery and gave testimony to a parliamentary committee.

From *An Account of the Slave Trade on the Coast of Africa*, Alexander Falconbridge, 1788.

so low that they became listless and weak. Some committed suicide.

Northern Europeans, such as the British, Danish, and French, soon led the slave trade, which at first had been dominated by the Portuguese and Spanish. Those who profited from slavery included plantation owners and sugar brokers. Seaports such as Bristol and Liverpool in England, and Nantes, La Rochelle, and Lorient in France, became rich from the slave trade.

A wretched landing

To many later immigrants to the New World, the Americas offered hope for the future and an escape from poverty or oppression. To millions of Africans, it was just the opposite. Their arrival was a moment of utter despair.

The destinations of the slave ships varied over the years. Many sailed to Portuguese-ruled Brazil, or to the Spanish colonies in Central and South America. Many went to other colonies in the region, ruled by Britain, France, Denmark, and the Netherlands. These were located in the Caribbean islands (then known as the West Indies) and in northeastern South America. Slaves were also traded onward from one New World location to another.

At first, the European colonies in North America (the lands that would later become the United States of America) took fewer slaves than South America and the Caribbean. The North American workforce in the early colonial period was supported by unpaid indentured laborers or apprentices, who were shipped over from Europe at the employer's cost. They were released from their obligations when the contract expired. However, during the 1600s, more and more African slaves began to replace this source of labor. Many of the slaves were put to work in the southern colonies, where tobacco and cotton were being grown on plantations.

Slaves could be presold by merchants, or publicly auctioned on arrival. They could be bought or sold again in this way throughout their lives.

SOURCE

ADVERTISEMENT

"TO BE SOLD AND LET by Public Auction on Monday eighteenth May 1829, under the trees. For sale, the three following SLAVES viz. HANNIBAL, about 30 Years Old, an excellent House Servant, of Good Character, WILLIAM, about 35 years old, a Laborer, NANCY, an excellent House Servant and Nurse. …

Also for sale, at Eleven o'Clock, Fine Rice, Gram, Paddy, Books, Muslins, Needles, Pins, Ribbons &c. &c. …
At One o'Clock that celebrated English horse Blucher."

The humans are on sale as chattels, in the same category as food, household goods, and horses.

Bill announcing a slave auction, Jamaica, 1829.

Slaves stand on the auction block in the southern United States in 1861, at the outbreak of the American Civil War. A mother cradles her baby anxiously.

Families including small children were often split up, never to see each other again. Slaves who were in a poor or sick condition were sold for very little. Those being sold faced a humiliating physical examination to determine their health, as purchasers examined their teeth or the condition of their muscles. They could then be branded with the emblem or initials of their new "owners."

A first priority of the owners was to break the spirit and identity of the newcomers. Their African names were replaced with European ones. They were taught their new duties and introduced to hard labor. Some slave owners were fairer than others, but the newcomers' introduction to life as a slave was often marked by bullying, beating, and extreme punishment, resulting in many deaths.

Economics of slave labor

The work undertaken by slaves varied greatly. A few might work as household servants, responsible for cooking, cleaning, child care, or maintenance. Other slaves might look after herds of cattle—work that many new arrivals would have been familiar with back in Africa. Some might work in mines or mills or forges. Skilled laborers, such as carpenters, fetched a high price at auctions.

The greatest number of slaves in the New World worked on plantations. These large farming estates, often of 865 acres (350 hectares) or more, were given over to a single cash crop, such as sugar, coffee, tobacco, indigo, or cotton. Before the invention of new farm machinery in the nineteenth century, production on plantations was labor intensive—many people had to do large amounts of physical work. This might include clearing land, weeding, sowing, harvesting, and processing. The produce of plantations would generally be exported to the ruling colonial powers, either as a raw material (such as American cotton) or as a finished product or by-product (for example, Jamaican sugar, molasses, and rum).

Slaves pick cotton in the state of Mississippi, in the 1880s. New technology boosted cotton production at this time, and by 1850, nearly three-quarters of all U.S. slaves worked in the cotton industry.

Profits enriched owners and investors back in Europe, but were of little benefit to local economic development. The life of African slaves was cheap. Some owners claimed that it was cheaper for owners to increase output by working slaves to death and buying replacements, than to care for their welfare. Many slaves could not expect to live much beyond 40 years.

Slavery skewed the economy in many ways, for instance, by keeping the wages of free workers low and by adding costs to society, such as the enforcement of slavery laws. A period of major political and economic change in the Americas began with the American Revolution (1775–83).

An auction of "field hands" (slaves used to working on the land) is advertised in the city of New Orleans in 1840.

BOOK

"The experience of all ages and nations, I believe, demonstrates that the work done by slaves, though it appears to cost only their maintenance, is in the end the dearest of any. A person who can acquire no property can have no other interest but to eat as much and to labor as little as possible. Whatever work he does beyond what is sufficient to purchase his own maintenance, can be squeezed out of him by violence only, and not by any interest of his own."

Adam Smith was a Scottish economist who argued against the slave trade on economic grounds.

From *The Wealth of Nations*, Chapter 2, Adam Smith, 1776.

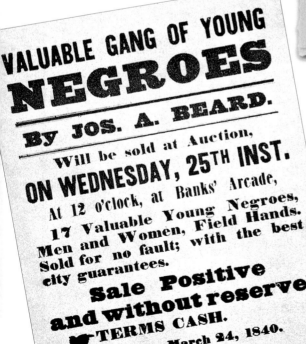

VALUABLE GANG OF YOUNG
NEGROES
By JOS. A. BEARD.
Will be sold at Auction,
ON WEDNESDAY, 25TH INST.
At 12 o'clock, at Banks' Arcade,
17 Valuable Young Negroes,
Men and Women, Field Hands.
Sold for no fault; with the best
city guarantees.
Sale Positive
and without reserve!
TERMS CASH.
New Orleans, March 24, 1840.

As a result of this conflict, North America's British colonies broke away to form an independent nation, the United States of America (U.S.A.). The breaking of colonial ties was followed by industrialization in the northern states of the new country, while the southern states continued with the old plantation economy. These events would greatly affect the future of slavery.

Living and working

A plantation owner would live in a grand house. In hot climates, this would be built on higher ground to catch cool breezes. High ground was also easier to defend against a slave rebellion. The plantation included housing for the overseers, barns, offices, a smithy (a blacksmith's workshop), workshops, and mills.

would be issued with only basic clothing. Food might include cornmeal or salt fish, or vegetables grown in plots.

The plantation was a community apart. Men, women, and children as young as four or five worked long

SOURCE

ACCOUNT

This is an Antislavery Tract and was published in Liverpool. It described the trade as "*horrible and inhuman.*" The tract criticizes the mistreatment of slaves and the use of "iron instruments" by slave owners.

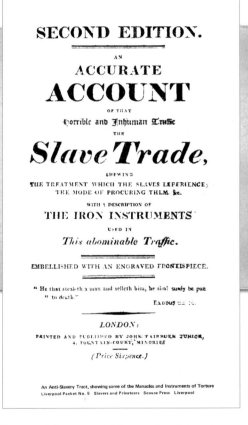

SECOND EDITION.

AN

ACCURATE

ACCOUNT

OF THAT

horrible and Inhuman Traffic

THE

Slave Trade,

SHEWING

THE TREATMENT WHICH THE SLAVES EXPERIENCE;
THE MODE OF PROCURING THEM. &c.

WITH A DESCRIPTION OF

THE IRON INSTRUMENTS

USED IN

This abominable Traffic.

EMBELLISHED WITH AN ENGRAVED FRONTISPIECE.

" He that steai th a man and selleth him, he shal surely be put
" to death."

EXODUS xxi. 10.

LONDON:

PRINTED AND PUBLISHED BY JOHN FAIRBURN JUNIOR,
4, FOUNTAIN-COURT, MINORIES

(Price Sixpence.)

An Anti-Slavery Tract, showing some of the Manacles and Instruments of Torture
Liverpool Packet No. 5 Slavers and Privateers Scouse Press Liverpool

Slaves lived in small huts, sited at some distance from the big house. Dwellings were hot in warm weather, draughty in cold weather, and muddy when it rained. Each hut might be shared by about ten individuals. Living conditions varied over time and from one region to another. In many places, there was just a bare earth floor on which to sleep, and a ragged blanket for keeping warm at night. Slaves

hours. They would be pushed hard and risked being whipped if they fell behind. Slaves could not marry without the owner's permission. Female slaves might be raped or abused. There was no education for children or adults, and organized meetings were forbidden. In many colonies, owners were protected by special legal codes (groups of laws). These denied slaves the most basic rights.

Despite such treatment, slaves somehow managed to keep their values and sense of pride. They raised their spirits with old folk tales from Africa, often fables about cunning animals that played tricks on each other. Some African languages survived and mixed with French, Dutch or English to form new languages, referred to as Creole. Slaves sang and beat out the rhythms of African music—even though drumming was sometimes banned because overseers feared it contained coded signals for an uprising. Today's popular Afro-American and Afro-Caribbean music (such as gospel, blues, jazz, and reggae) can be traced back to the African traditions.

African beliefs in gods and spirits also survived, despite often being forbidden. Some traditions were brought from West Africa and continue today in rituals called Vodun in Haiti and Candomblé in Brazil. Plantation owners were at first reluctant to let slaves become Christians, for fear that the religion would give them hope or ideas of equality. However, in the 1800s, Christianity spread rapidly among slaves.

BOOK

"These overseers are indeed for the most part persons of the worst character. … They pay no regard to the situation of pregnant women, nor the least attention to the lodging of the field-negroes. Their huts … are often open sheds, built in damp places; so that when the poor creatures return tired from the toils of the field, they contract many disorders."

Olaudah Equiano, a freed slave who campaigned against slavery, describes plantation life in the Caribbean.

From *The Interesting Narrative of the Life of Olaudah Equiano, or Gustavus Vassa, The African*, Chapter 5, Olaudah Equiano, 1789.

Olaudah Equiano traveled far and wide campaigning against slavery (see page 19).

Freedom, escape, and rebellion

In the U.S.A., there were free people of African or mixed racial descent as well as slaves. Some had been there since the early colonial period and owned houses and businesses. Some bought and owned slaves themselves. Manumission could be purchased, or the owner could grant it willingly. For most slaves, the chances of manumission remained small. Their only route to freedom was resistance, escape, or revolt. Most fugitive slaves were recaptured and punished.

However, even as early as the 1500s, some slaves succeeded in escaping. Some fled ashore from wrecked slave ships, others disappeared into the countryside. In the 1600s, some fugitive slaves joined the crews of pirate ships. In Cuba, Jamaica, Haiti, Dominica,

St. Vincent, and Surinam, escaped slaves known as Maroons fled to the mountains or the forest, founding villages and living by hunting and farming. They raided plantations and stole cattle. In both Jamaica and Surinam, there were long wars in the eighteenth century between Maroons and the colonial authorities.

During that period, slave rebellions broke out in Jamaica, Guyana, Curaçao, and Venezuela. The most effective uprising was in Haiti, from 1791 to

PRESS REPORT

"At Port-au-Prince, and in the environs, the Negroes are in a state of insurrection [rebellion]; they have burnt many habitations, which had remained untouched till this day. The Negroes will not work. On this side of Grand Rivière, there is a great rising."

This was one of several conflicting reports about the slaves' revolution in Haiti (then known as Saint-Domingue) published in the press.

This report was in the *Pennsylvania Gazette* on September 28, 1796, based on an article that had first appeared in the *Courier Française* on August 23, 1796.

Slaves rise up against French plantation owners and their families, setting fire to Plaine du Cap on the Caribbean island territory of Haiti (Saint-Domingue) in 1794. Haiti would become the first independent black state in the Caribbean.

1804. The colonial power was France, which was itself in a revolutionary state at that time. Haitian slaves killed French settlers and burned the hated sugar plantations. The rebellion developed into a complex war, eventually involving France, Spain, and Britain.

In 1792, France's revolutionary government agreed to make all colonial peoples, black or white, equal citizens. The general of the Haitian rebels, a former slave known as Toussaint l'Ouverture, could now support France. However, when Toussaint declared his intention of ruling Haiti, he was tricked into being sent to France, where he died in prison. The French now planned to reintroduce slavery, but in 1803, the Haitians defeated their army. In 1804, Haiti became independent under the rule of former slave Jean-Jacques Dessalines.

Following the Haitian uprising, rebellions broke out across the Americas—in Brazil, Barbados, Jamaica, and Guyana.

In the United States, there were repeated attempts at insurrection. Gabriel Prosser's plans for an uprising in 1800 were foiled, as were Denmark Vesey's in 1822. A violent uprising in Virginia, led by Nat Turner in 1831, was suppressed violently, with widespread killings of revenge.

SOURCE

ENGRAVING

An early nineteenth-century engraving of Toussaint l'Ouverture on horseback.

"Am I not a Man and a Brother?"

Human rights are the basic principles of liberty and justice that most people would wish to experience in their lives. In the eighteenth century, leading European writers began to discuss human rights. These thinkers included the French philosopher, Jean-Jacques Rousseau (1712–78), and the English-born political activist, Thomas Paine (1737–1809). Their ideas about liberty were applied by many people to the debate about slavery.

Although supporters of slavery could quote the scriptures of the Bible in support of their case, more and more Christians were becoming concerned about the human misery involved in the trades involving slaves.

At the forefront of new antislavery campaigns were the Quakers, a Christian movement that dedicated itself to peace, justice, and equality. In the United Kingdom, a legal ruling of 1772 effectively made slavery illegal within England and Wales, and a similar ruling was made in the Scottish courts in 1778.

The next priority was to bring an end to the shameful trade overseas. A Society for Effecting the Abolition of the Slave Trade was founded in 1787. Leading campaigners included James Ramsay, Thomas Clarkson, and Hannah More.

SOURCE

MEDALLION

The motto for the Society for Effecting the Abolition of the Slave Trade was "*Am I not a Man and a Brother?*" This medallion was designed in 1787 by the famous English potter, Josiah Wedgewood.

A well-known politician named William Wilberforce led the campaign in Parliament.

Freed slaves played a major part in the campaign. One of the most remarkable was Olaudah Equiano (see page 15), who campaigned not just against slavery but for voting rights for all British citizens. He wrote a moving account of his life as a slave. Historians have questioned some details of his early life, but he made the case against slavery very powerfully.

The Slave Trade Act of 1807 ended the slave trade in British colonies, but it was not until 1833 that the United Kingdom Parliament abolished the condition of slavery altogether. Campaigns against the international trade were continued by the British and Foreign antislavery Society formed in 1839.

Other European powers also moved toward full abolition. Denmark achieved this in 1802. In France, campaigners had founded *La Société des Amis des Noirs* (Society for the Friends of Blacks) in 1788. In 1794, following the uprising in Haiti, the revolutionary government passed a decree of Universal Emancipation for slaves in all French colonies. However, this was repealed when Napoleon took power in France. Lasting abolition finally occurred in 1848. The Brazilians, whose Portuguese ancestors had started the slave trade in the 1400s, finally abolished slavery in 1888.

SPEECH

"As soon as ever I had arrived thus far in my investigation of the slave trade, I confess to you, sir, so enormous, so dreadful, so irremediable did its wickedness appear that my own mind was completely made up for the abolition. A trade founded in iniquity, and carried on as this was, must be abolished, let the policy be what it might, let the consequences be what they would, I from this time determined that I would never rest till I had effected its abolition."

William Wilberforce (shown above) was true to the words of this speech. He died just three days before the full Slavery Abolition Act was passed in 1833.

William Wilberforce MP, speech to the House of Commons in favor of the Abolition of the Slave Trade, May 12, 1789.

Return to Africa

In 1787, a city named Freetown was founded in Sierra Leone, in West Africa. It was intended as a new home for various people of African descent living in Britain and North America. Some of these had been freed from slavery as a reward for fighting on the British side during the American Revolution (1775–83). There were poor blacks from the streets of London and a group of freed slaves, who had previously been resettled in Nova Scotia, Canada. A later group was made up of Jamaican Maroons, who had first been deported to Nova Scotia after the Second Maroon War of 1795.

The settlers in Sierra Leone endured many difficulties, including disease and hostility from the indigenous peoples and quarrels among the organizers. The governing Sierra Leone Company's refusal to grant settlers full rights led to a rebellion in 1799. Descendants of the Freetown settlers became known as Creoles, speakers of the Krio

SOURCE

MOTTO

"The Love of Liberty Brought Us Here."
The national motto of Liberia recalls the reason the nation was founded.

The first 400 settlers in Freetown, in Sierra Leone, were soon joined by other liberated slaves, whose ancestors had originally been taken from many different parts of Africa.

language. This language developed through a mixing of African and European languages.

Antislavery campaigners in the U.S.A. also became interested in African resettlement. In 1822, the American Colonization Society set up a similar venture in a neighboring territory they named Liberia (from the Latin word *liber*, meaning "free"). An independent Republic of Liberia was declared in 1847. The project was criticized by some, who felt that it played into the hands of whites who wished to expel African Americans from the U.S.A. The many freed slaves who came to Liberia prospered but failed to integrate with the indigenous peoples. They formed a separate, powerful pro-American elite.

From 1808 to 1860, Sierra Leone also served as a base from which British naval patrols could enforce prohibition of the transatlantic slave trade. The U.K.'s government made a series of treaties with foreign nations. These enabled the British to intercept and arrest slavers at sea. Britain, which had helped create the transatlantic trade, now set about ending it.

Britain's overseas empire was also spreading into East Africa at this time.

The Scottish explorer and missionary, David Livingstone, made public the appalling cruelties of the East African slave traders. As a result, the U.K. persuaded the Sultan of Zanzibar to close down the big slave market on the island in 1873, bringing the East African trade to an end.

Joseph Jenkins Roberts was the son of a free African American from Virginia. He became independent Liberia's first president in 1848.

SOURCE

NAVAL ORDERS

"You are to use every means in your power to prevent a continuance of the traffic in slaves and to give full effect to the Acts of Parliament in question …"

These were the orders, to Sir George Collier, Commodore (an officer in the navy) of Britain's West African Squadron, 1818–21. Collier patrolled the West African coast with six antislavery vessels. The owners of captured slave ships could be taken back to Sierra Leone and tried in court.

Slavery by any other name

The abolition of slavery did not bring to an end the economic system of the age, which was imperialist (based on empires). Powerful European nations still colonized the rest of the world in order to control resources and raw materials, and create new markets for the goods they manufactured. The profits continued to go back to investors in Europe.

Colonial workers may have been freed from slavery, but they were living in extreme poverty. Caribbean islanders still had to toil in the cane fields, or try to make a living by growing vegetables and fishing.

South Sea Islanders, known as Kanaka, work the pineapple fields of Queensland, Australia, in the 1890s. Terms of work varied greatly. Some were voluntary economic migrants, others were indentured laborers.

After abolition, plantation owners around the world began to turn to other forms of unfree labor, such as indenture. Overseas workers were contracted to work for the same employer for a fixed period, with wretched conditions of employment.

India, then under British rule, was

BOOK

"… he was tied to a gun and flogged; he had a great number of lashes given to him, I think very nearly fifty. … The man shrieked a little and drew up his body; and I heard the Provost-marshall (officer in charge of military police in a camp or city), Mr. Ramsay, say, 'Take down that man and hang him.'"

Colonial brutality continued long after the abolition of slavery in the British empire. In 1865, poor Jamaicans petitioned for the right to plant crops on government-owned land. The request was refused, sparking off an uprising that was fiercely suppressed. The leader of the rebellion, Paul Bogle, was killed along with 439 blacks, in what became known as the Morant Bay Rebellion. A sympathetic politician, George William Gordon, was hanged.

From *The Reign of Terror: A Narrative of Facts concerning ex-Governor Eyre, George William Gordon and the Jamaica Atrocities*, Henry Bleby, 1868.

a major new source of indentured labor. Colonies that made use of this type of workforce included Mauritius and Réunion in the Indian Ocean,

South Africa, Trinidad, and other Caribbean islands, Guyana and Surinam in South America, and Fiji in the Pacific. Some Australian Aborigines and many Pacific islanders were also used as indentured laborers, in Queensland, Australia. Although some entered into contracts willingly, many were tricked, kidnapped, or pressed into employment by illegal human traffickers, nicknamed "blackbirders."

In the late nineteenth century, European nations competed to colonize almost all of Africa, which they did not yet control. This period became known as the "Scramble for Africa." Although this helped to end formal slavery, it also forced oppressive working conditions on many Africans.

One of the worst examples was in the Congo Free State (1885–1908), which was run as a personal colony by King Leopold II of Belgium. African workers were forced onto Belgian rubber plantations and violently punished if they failed to meet production quotas (the amount of produce they needed to provide within a certain time). Workers were terrorized, murdered, mutilated, and raped. Amid international outcry, the Belgian government finally took over the running of the colony in 1908.

In late nineteenth century and early twentieth century, many colonial peoples founded nationalist

A photograph from Jamaica, taken in about 1880, shows cane-cutters chewing on sticks of sugarcane. In the slave era, Jamaica produced over one-fifth of the world's sugar. After the slaves were freed, crops such as bananas and coffee became increasingly important on the island.

movements in order to campaign for economic justice, civil rights, and independence. Civil rights are the basic human rights that all people deserve within a country, such as the right to vote, the right to free speech, or the right to live without servitude. The struggle to gain these freedoms would take many descendents of slaves and colonial peoples over a hundred years to achieve. Many would say that the struggle still goes on today.

American campaigns

The American Declaration of Independence of 1776 stated, *"We hold these truths to be self-evident, that all men are created equal."* However, the new nation's founding fathers included slave owners as well as many active opponents of slavery. Failure to settle the question of slavery at this point led to later conflict. Abolition movements did grow rapidly in the early years. Slavery was gradually banned in the northern states in

Harriet Tubman (ca. 1820–1913) helped hundreds of slaves escape to freedom.

LETTER

"The movements were almost always made in the night, and the fugitives were taken from one station to another by wagon and sometimes by foot; they consisted of old men and young, women, children, and nursing babes. Sometimes they came singly, sometimes by the dozen. In the middle of the night, there came a low knock on the door, a window was raised softly—'Who is there?' a low, well-known voice in reply—'How many?' The next day (or sometimes many days), and then on an auspicious night, forwarded to the next station. Clothing is changed where possible, fetters removed where necessary; wounds are dressed, hungry bodies fed; weary limbs are rested, fainting hearts strengthened, and then up again and away for Canada."

This letter recalls the "Underground Railroad" by which perhaps as many as 30,000 fugitive slaves escaped from the southern states.

Extract from a letter by Dr. Edwin Fussell, written in 1880, reprinted in *History of the Underground Railroad in Chester and the Neighboring Counties of Pennsylvania*, Robert C. Smedley, 1883.

the years between 1780 and 1804. The southern states, where the economy was reliant on cotton plantations, still supported slavery.

Importing new slaves into the U.S.A. was banned in 1808, although local trading in slaves remained legal in the South. Many blacks and whites took up the cause of total abolition. In 1831, William Lloyd Garrison founded an influential newspaper called *The Liberator*. He set up the American Antislavery Society in 1832. Another tireless campaigner was Frederick Douglass (1818–95), himself an escaped slave.

The case against slavery was boosted in 1839 when African slaves held on board a Spanish schooner (sailing vessel), *Amistad*, mutinied and seized control. They decided to sail for Africa, but their ship was brought into New York. In the court case that followed, it was ruled that the slaves should go free. Times were changing.

The abolition movement was supported by many Christian groups, especially the Quakers, but opposed by some. It was closely allied with the movement for women's rights, a link that caused controversy at the time. One effective campaigner in both causes was an eloquent ex-slave named Sojourner Truth (1797–1883).

Another was Harriet Tubman, a slave who escaped in 1849. In the years that followed, she helped organize the secret escape routes (nicknamed the "Underground Railroad") from the slave-owning Southern states to the northern states and Canada.

The most radical abolitionist was John Brown, a white man who believed that only armed force could bring about liberation. In 1859, he led a successful raid on an armory in Harper's Ferry, West Virginia, but was captured and hanged.

SOURCE

POSTER

Uncle Tom's Cabin (1852) was an antislavery novel by a teacher named Harriet Beecher Stowe. It was written in the sentimental style of its time, and the racial stereotyping of characters such as Uncle Tom was mocked by later generations of African Americans. However, the book became an international bestseller and played a huge part in winning support for abolition. This is a poster advertising the book.

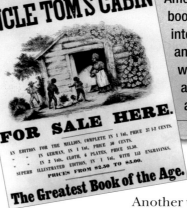

135,000 SETS, 270,000 VOLUMES SOLD.

UNCLE TOM'S CABIN

FOR SALE HERE.

AN EDITION FOR THE MILLION, COMPLETE IN 1 Vol., PRICE 37 1-2 CENTS.
" " IN GERMAN, IN 1 Vol., PRICE 50 CENTS.
" " IN 2 Vols., CLOTH, 6 PLATES, PRICE $1.50.
SUPERB ILLUSTRATED EDITION, IN 1 Vol., WITH 153 ENGRAVINGS,
PRICES FROM $2.50 TO $5.00.

The Greatest Book of the Age.

The American Civil War

In 1857, a legal ruling (in the case of an African American named Dred Scott) caused an uproar. It implied that people of African descent could not be regarded as full citizens of the U.S.A., and that the U.S. Congress did not have federal powers to prohibit slavery. Abolitionists were outraged. As more and more western land was being absorbed into the nation, this opened up the prospect of slavery being extended far and wide.

The Southerners had different fears. As the northern states became industrialized, more and more Europeans were pouring in to work in northeastern factories. Southerners were being outnumbered politically and overtaken economically.

In 1860, Abraham Lincoln won the race to be the Republican candidate in the U.S. presidential election. Lincoln was known to have antislavery views, but when Southern states threatened to secede (withdraw) from the Union, he promised not to interfere with slavery in the states where it existed. However, seven slave-owning states did secede to form a southern Confederacy, and as a result a full-scale civil war broke out in 1861. Four more states now joined the Confederacy against the Union.

The American Civil War was fought principally about the relationship between federal government and state government— although this issue was, of course, tied up with slavery, too. Lincoln feared that slave-owning

A brighter future for Isaac and Rosa, emancipated in 1863.

ISAAC and ROSA, Emancipated Slave Children,
From the Free Schools of Louisiana, N.Y.
Photographed by KIMBALL, 477 Broadway. N.Y.
Entered according to Act of Congress, in the year 1863 by GEO. H.
Clerk's Office of the U. S. for the Sou. Dist. of N.Y.

allies would switch to the Confederate cause, and so it was only in 1862 that he felt bold enough to confirm the abolition of slavery as a major goal of the war. Lincoln proclaimed the emancipation of all slaves in the Confederate areas, and was re-elected two years later.

African-American regiments were raised to fight for the Union and played a major part in the fighting. The war was a bloody conflict, fought with great bitterness. It was very costly in terms of money and lives, leaving hundreds of thousands dead. Early photography recorded the fighting, so we still have a moving record of the tragedy, its troops, and its weaponry.

African Americans join the fight for the Union. E Company of the 4th U.S. Colored Infantry prepares to march at Fort Lincoln, Maryland.

By 1865, the war had been won by the Union. The Confederacy was defeated and lay in ruins. In April of that year, Lincoln was assassinated by an embittered Southerner named John Wilkes Booth.

SOURCE

SONG

"John Brown's body lies a-moldering in the grave, (x3)
His soul is marching on!

Chorus
Glory, halle-hallelujah! Glory, halle-hallelujah!
Glory, halle-hallelujah! His soul is marching on!

He's gone to be a soldier in the army of the Lord, (x3)
His soul is marching on!

John Brown's knapsack is strapped to his back, (x3)
His soul is marching on!

They will hang Jeff Davis to a sour apple tree (x3)
As they march along!

Now, three rousing cheers for the Union, (x3)
As we are marching on!"

John Brown, the radical opponent of slavery (see page 25), had been executed two years before the Civil War. He was a hero to many abolitionists. He featured in the most famous song of the Civil War, popular with Union troops as they marched to battle. Jeff(erson) Davis was President of the Confederacy.

These are selected verses from the song *John Brown's Body*.

The Jim Crow years

The abolition of slavery in the United States was at last confirmed in the 13th Amendment to the Constitution, passed in 1865. The new president, Andrew Johnson, was a Southerner who had supported Lincoln. He oversaw Reconstruction in the South, a period during which Southern legislatures were forced to accept the 13th Amendment. However, Johnson had no interest in African Americans

Whites glare as an African American votes in the 1867 mayoral election in Georgetown, DC. A white equal rights candidate, Charles D. Welch, was voted in with black support.

winning further rights. Even when the U.S. Congress introduced a 14th Amendment (1868) granting African Americans full citizenship, Southern legislatures continued to enforce a two-tier legal system based on color. These groups of racist laws were known as Black Codes.

In 1869, former Unionist general Ulysses S. Grant became president. Under the 15th Amendment (1870), African Americans at last won the right to vote. The 14th and 15th Amendments were now pushed through the Southern legislatures during a second phase, known as "Radical Reconstruction," which lasted until 1877. Black people were now able to vote in state government and Congress elections, and for a time, did so.

However, many white Southerners could not bear to see former slaves being treated as their equals. Southern legislatures began to pass new laws with the sole aim of preventing black people voting or standing for state government. Some laws insisted that voters be able to read and write. Since education for slaves had been banned in the era of slavery, this was clearly unfair. Poll taxes were introduced, which had to be paid before voting. This excluded many poor blacks. Other laws brought in segregation, the division of public services and places with the aim of keeping the races apart. All these measures are often referred to as Jim Crow laws, named after a stereotyped black character in racist minstrel shows that began in the 1830s.

The political problems of African Americans were made worse by grinding poverty. Many former slaves—and poor whites, too—worked as sharecroppers. Landowners allowed them to use a plot of land for farming, in return for a share of the crop. This left the sharecropper with little profit.

This engraving was produced in 1870 and is entitled **The Result of the Fifteenth Amendment.** *The right of African Americans to vote was a major political advance, but further laws had to be passed before it became a reality.*

U.S. CONSTITUTION

"The right of citizens of the United States to vote shall not be denied or abridged by the United States or by any State on account of race, color, or previous condition of servitude."

The 15th Amendment to the Constitution of the United States in 1870 could not be clearer. However, it was ignored, hindered, and bypassed until the passing of the Voting Rights Act in 1965 (see page 37).

Racism and prejudice

Racism starts with the belief that human beings are divided into genetic groups (races), which are significantly different from each other. It goes on to make the assumption that some groups are superior to others. Such notions were reinforced by the African slave trade and by imperialism. Many white colonists and rulers were ignorant of the culture and history of the peoples they governed. They considered other races, especially Africans, to be their inferiors. Ignorance was coupled with fear that their subjects would rise up against them. There was a sharp rise in racism around the world in the late nineteenth and early twentieth centuries.

In the U.S.A., many whites and blacks worked patiently to overcome prejudice. The educationalist, Booker T. Washington (1856–1915), of the Tuskegee Institute in Alabama, sought a solution in economic advance, teaching young blacks useful trades. W. E. B. Du Bois, publications director of the National Association for the Advancement of Colored People (NAACP), founded in 1909, used legal challenges to campaign for complete equality.

Some poor whites in the U.S.A. feared economic competition from free, educated African Americans. After the Civil War, an extreme racist organization called the Ku Klux Klan had grown up in the South. It was revived in 1915. Its white members disguised themselves in robes and

Ku Klux Klan members parade at the funeral of a police officer in Madison, Wisconsin, in 1924. Many police and public officials supported the KKK.

hoods, and terrorized African American families by burning, bullying, and lynching them. Between 1919 and 1925, perhaps a million blacks left the violence and poverty of the South to seek work in the factories of northern cities such as Chicago.

In Europe, after World War I ended in 1918, racism became embedded in extreme political movements. The German National Socialists, or Nazis, believed that Jewish people and Roma (a traveling people who originally came from India and are sometimes referred to as gypsies)were subhuman. In Germany, these people were first deprived of civil rights, then forced into slave labor and murdered in death camps.

The Nazi leader, Adolf Hitler, also despised people of African descent, even banning music with roots in black culture, such as jazz. When Germany hosted the Olympic Games in Berlin in 1936, Hitler intended them to showcase the superiority of his "race." Unfortunately for him, a fine African-American athlete named Jesse Owens, who won four gold medals, dominated the games. Owens, grandson of a slave and son of a sharecropper, had experienced plenty of prejudice back home. In Berlin, he showed how the human spirit could rise above racism.

Jesse Owens (1913–80) was the African-American star of the Berlin Olympics in 1936.

SOURCE

ENCYCLOPEDIA

"The negro would appear to stand on a lower evolutionary plane than the white man, and to be more closely related to the higher anthropoids. ... Mentally, the negro is inferior to the white."

This is the entry for "Negro" in *Encyclopedia Britannica Volume 19, 13th Edition*, 1926. Extreme racist views were very widespread in the 1920s. The statement above was not made by the Ku Klux Klan or the Nazis, but was represented as "fact" in a respected and best-selling encyclopedia. This false definition is not acceptable today.

Segregation and the state

Racism may be created by vague fears, heated emotion, and blind ignorance, but when it is transformed into a country's laws, it becomes detailed and precise in its oppressiveness.

In the U.S.A., racist legislation such as the Jim Crow laws deprived the black population of its civil rights, its ability to participate in society or contribute to it. Segregation laws and customs divided people at every stage of daily life. A young black man could not date or marry a white girl. Blacks and whites could not eat in the same restaurants, go to the same school or dance hall, share the same water fountain, use the same elevators or changing rooms.

A Civil Rights Act had been passed in 1875 to prevent such injustices, but it was never seriously enforced and was challenged in law. Segregation even applied to U.S. troops serving overseas during World Wars I and II. The barriers created by segregation served only to perpetuate and reinforce the ignorance of both black and white people about each other.

Segregation was found in many other parts of the world, too, and was not just directed against those of African descent, but against Asians,

During World War II (1939–45), the U.S.A. stationed African-American troops in England, where there was no racial segregation in public places.

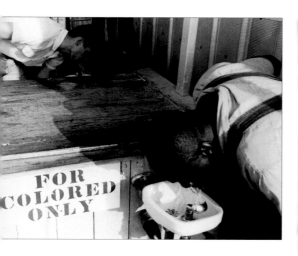

Segregation in the southern U.S.A.—there is one water fountain for whites, another for blacks.

SPEECH

"The white man makes all the laws, he drags us before his courts and accuses us, and he sits in judgement over us. It is fit and proper to raise the question sharply, what is this rigid color-bar in the administration of justice? … I feel oppressed by the atmosphere of white domination that lurks all around in this courtroom. Somehow this atmosphere calls to mind the inhuman injustices caused to my people outside this courtroom by this same white domination."

This speech was by Nelson Mandela as he faced a South African court in 1962. Mandela was accused of inciting an illegal strike and of leaving the country without a valid passport. He attacks the "color-bar" (racial discrimination), which was the essence of South Africa in the apartheid era.

Australian Aborigines, Native Americans, and many other peoples. In the overseas empires of the British, French, and Dutch, native peoples were commonly excluded from many activities and locations.

From 1948 to 1990, Afrikaners, descendants of Dutch settlers in South Africa, created a whole state based on segregation laws. They called the system apartheid, meaning "separation." Although the great majority of the population were black Africans, they were forced to live in certain areas, made to carry passes at all times, refused good jobs, and were unable to vote. Asians, mainly the descendants of indentured laborers, were classed in a separate restricted group, known as Coloreds.

The injustices in South Africa were challenged by a brave band of campaigners, both black and white, just as slavery had been challenged a century or two earlier. The most famous opponent of apartheid was Nelson Mandela (born in 1918), who served 27 years in jail. The system collapsed in 1991 when Frederick W. de Klerk repealed apartheid laws. Mandela was elected as South Africa's first black president in 1994.

"Winds of change"

Nazi Germany was defeated in 1945, at the end of World War II. This was a major setback for racist politics. A new international treaty organization, the United Nations (UN), was founded in the same year. In 1948, it issued a Universal Declaration of Human Rights, which dealt with many of the historical injustices associated with the slave trade. It did not prevent them from happening, but it clearly set out the basic principles of justice.

The first postwar immigrants from Jamaica arrive in England on board a ship called the **Empire Windrush,** *in 1948.*

At this time, the economics of empire were changing. The U.S.A. was now the richest nation in the world. Europe, exhausted by two world wars, was bankrupt. Its colonies were demanding independence. In some places, power was handed over peacefully. In others, there were bloody conflicts between nationalist or communist insurgents and colonial powers. In India, an activist named Mohandas K. Gandhi campaigned for independence from British rule by pioneering nonviolent methods of protest, such as refusing to pay certain taxes.

India became independent in 1947. Ghana, one of the regions of West Africa devastated by the slave trade, became independent in 1957. In 1960, the British prime minister, Harold Macmillan, acknowledged that a *"wind of change"* was blowing across the African continent. In the Caribbean, Jamaica and Trinidad became independent in 1962.

The fortunes of the newly independent nations were mixed. Some thrived under democratic governments. Others had been weakened by centuries of neglect. Their problems were soon compounded by corruption, dictatorship, and military rule. Many new nations were sucked into

UNIVERSAL DECLARATION OF HUMAN RIGHTS

Article 1. All human beings are born free and equal in dignity and rights. They are endowed with reason and conscience and should act toward one another in a spirit of brotherhood.

Article 2. Everyone is entitled to all the rights and freedoms set forth in this Declaration, without distinction of any kind, such as race, color, sex, language, religion, political or other opinion, national or social origin, property, birth, or other status. Furthermore, no distinction shall be made on the basis of the political, jurisdictional, or international status of the country or territory to which a person belongs, whether it be independent, trust, non-self-governing, or under any other limitation of sovereignty.

Article 3. Everyone has the right to life, liberty, and security of person.

Article 4. No one shall be held in slavery or servitude; slavery and the slave trade shall be prohibited in all their forms.

Article 5. No one shall be subjected to torture or to cruel, inhuman, or degrading treatment or punishment.

These are the first five articles of the Declaration that provided the guidelines for nations in the modern world.

United Nations [Organization], 1948.

conflicting loyalties during the Cold War (1945–90). This was a period of tension between the Western powers, dominated by the U.S.A., and the communist powers, dominated by the Soviet Union and China. Other new nations chose to remain nonaligned. The old empires may have vanished, but international power struggles and trading systems that favored the world's richest nations suggested that imperialism was not yet dead.

Many people from the world's poorer nations now sought work in the homelands of the old colonial rulers. Immigrants came to France from North Africa, to the Netherlands from Surinam and Indonesia, and to the United Kingdom from the Caribbean and Asia. Many were descendants of the slaves and indentured laborers whose toil had made these empires rich in the past.

This movement of peoples brought a rich cultural diversity to Europe. Immigrants were sometimes treated well, but often faced new discrimination and racism.

"We shall overcome"

After 1945, the southern United States were still troubled by the Jim Crow laws and lynch mobs. In 1955, Emmett Till, an African-American teenager visiting Mississippi, whistled at a white woman and called her "baby." For this "crime," he was kidnapped, tortured, shot dead, and thrown in the river. When his murderers were put on trial, an all-white jury returned a verdict of "Not Guilty."

To oppose these racist actions, the NAACP, CORE (Congress of Racial Equality), and SNCC (the Student Nonviolent Coordinating Committee) organized civil rights activities. The civil rights movement aimed to abolish racial discrimination in the U.S.A. The organizations used nonviolent direct action. One area of protest concerned public transportation. In 1955, in Montgomery, Alabama, an African-American woman named Rosa Parks refused to give up her bus seat to a white man. She was arrested and fined. In protest, a bus boycott was started in the city. By the end of 1956, the U.S. Supreme Court had ruled that segregation on city buses was illegal. To challenge segregation on interstate buses, black and white protestors journeyed from Washington, DC to New Orleans in 1961. These freedom riders were fire-bombed and beaten.

Education was another priority. School segregation had been made

SOURCE

SPEECH

"I have a dream that one day this nation will rise up and live out the true meaning of its creed: 'We hold these truths to be self-evident: that all men are created equal.'

I have a dream that one day on the red hills of Georgia, the sons of former slaves and the sons of former slave owners will be able to sit down together at the table of brotherhood.

I have a dream that one day even the state of Mississippi, a state sweltering with the heat of injustice, sweltering with the heat of oppression, will be transformed into an oasis of freedom and justice.

I have a dream that my four little children will one day live in a nation where they will not be judged by the color of their skin but by the content of their character.

I have a dream today."

Dr. Martin Luther King Jr., speaking at the "March on Washington for Jobs and Freedom," August 28, 1963. The following year, he became the youngest man ever to be awarded the Nobel Peace Prize. He donated the money to the civil rights movement.

illegal in 1954, but the law was ignored. In 1957, there were riots in Little Rock, Arkansas, as crowds of whites tried to prevent black pupils from entering a high school. Troops had to be called in. In 1962, 3,000 federal troops were deployed to allow just one black student, James Meredith, to enrol in class at the University of Mississippi.

The civil rights movement was growing fast. Protest songs, such as "We Shall Overcome," became famous around the world. A campaign began to encourage African Americans to register for the vote. One of the activists was Medgar Evers of the NAACP. On June 12, 1963, he was shot dead in front of his home.

On August 28,1963, the dynamic leader of the civil rights movement, a Baptist minister named Dr. Martin Luther King, Jr., gave a moving speech to a crowd of 300,000 protestors in Washington, DC. But stormy times lay ahead. On November 22, 1963, the U.S. President, John F. Kennedy, was assassinated in Dallas, Texas. Protest marches continued amidst ongoing violence. John F. Kennedy had supported civil rights in his campaign, and although proposals had not always been followed through with legislation, the perception was that a progressive and youthful president had been cut down in his prime.

In 1965, a new Voting Rights Acts was passed, designed to enforce at last the 15th Amendment to the U.S. Constitution. In 1968, in a blow to the civil rights movement, Martin Luther King, too, was assassinated.

Dr. Martin Luther King (1929–68) was a great public speaker and a tireless campaigner for civil rights.

Black power

The civil rights movement in the southern United States was based on principles of nonviolence, equality, and moderation. However, for many years, some activists had engaged in more radical campaigns.

An organization called the Nation of Islam (NoI) had been founded in 1930. It did not adopt recognized Islamic teachings, but expressed views on religion, race, slavery, nationhood, freedom, and justice from a black perspective, calling for racial separation from whites. In the 1960s, many new followers were recruited by a powerful speaker named Malcolm X. ("X" represented the unknown African name of his ancestors before slavery).

In 1964, Malcolm X left the NoI, became an orthodox Muslim, and rejected black separatism.

Malcolm X was convinced that members of the NoI would retaliate because of his defection. Malcolm X's fears proved well-founded and he was murdered in 1965.

SOURCE

SPEECH

"We must begin to think politically and see if we can have the power to impose and keep the moral values that we hold high. We must question the values of this society, and I maintain that black people are the best people to do that, because we have been excluded from that society. And the question is, we ought to think whether or not we want to become a part of that society."

Stokely Carmichael (1941–1998, also known as Kwame Ture) was born in Trinidad and raised in the U.S.A. He was the chairman of the SNCC and became known as "Honorary Prime Minister" of the Black Panthers. He later moved to Africa.

Stokely Carmichael, speaking at Berkeley, California, 1966.

Malcolm X (1925–65) was one of the more radical and controversial voices to be heard in the U.S. civil rights struggle of the 1960s.

Another radical civil rights group was the Black Panther Party, formed in California in 1966, by Bobby Seale and Huey P. Newton. The Black Panthers were angry, armed, and militant and their cause became increasingly linked with revolutionary politics. Leading supporters such as Angela Davis went on to join the American Communist Party. Many different radical groups came together as strands of a broad movement that became known as Black Power.

This movement was born in the big cities of the northern and western states, where many African Americans lived in deprived areas known as ghettos. Racism and poverty were still rife. Housing was of low quality and unemployment and crime were high. In the "long, hot summers" of the late 1960s, the ghettos erupted with riots, burning, and looting.

In the Watts district of Los Angeles, a riot in 1965 left 36 dead and resulted in over $200 million-worth of damage. When Martin Luther King was murdered in 1968, rioting spread to one hundred American cities. At the Mexico Olympics that year, two African-American athletes gave the clenched-fist salute of Black Power.

The late 1960s was a time of youth rebellion and cultural change around the world. There were protests against America's war in Vietnam (1959–75). Black Power was part of this widespread rejection of traditional

SOURCE

BOOK

"I am America. I am the part you won't recognize. But get used to me. Black, confident, cocky; my name, not yours; my religion, not yours; my goals, my own; get used to me."

Muhammad Ali was born Cassius Clay in 1942, but changed his "slave" name during a period in the NoI. He was one of the world's greatest-ever boxers, three times winner of the World Heavyweight Championship.

From *The Greatest*, Muhammad Ali, 1975.

politics. It influenced attitudes in the Caribbean, in South America, in Africa, and in the cities of Europe. Black people now proclaimed pride in their heritage, in their dress and appearance, and in their music.

They had to decide the best way of achieving racial equality. Should they oppose the existing political system or work to succeed within it? Should government try to influence social behavior and popular attitudes with legislation? Laws could impose affirmative action—favoring disadvantaged candidates in job applications. These strategies are still hotly debated today.

African roots

A Jamaican named Marcus Garvey (1887–1940) was a campaigner, journalist, and businessman who in 1914 set up the Universal Negro Improvement Association and African Communities League (UNIA-ACL).

SPEECH

"Look for me in the whirlwind or the storm, look for me all around you, for, with God's grace, I shall come and bring with me countless millions of black slaves who have died in America and the West Indies and the millions in Africa to aid you in the fight for Liberty, Freedom, and Life."

Extract from *First Message to the Negroes of the World from Atlanta Prison*, Marcus Garvey, 1925.

Garvey's tactics were often controversial and sometimes condemned by other activists. For instance, Garvey was criticized when he talked with Edward Clarke of the racist group, the Ku Klux Klan, in 1922. However, his ideas were very influential. Garvey tried to forge links between the scattered peoples of African descent and the continent of

their ancestors. He wanted to engage them in the struggle against the colonial powers.

This policy, called Pan-Africanism, was advocated by many campaigners, including W. E. B. Du Bois (see page 30). The great African-American singer and actor, Paul Robeson (1898–1976) devoted himself to the struggle against racist lynching and segregation. He also helped to found a Council on African Affairs in 1937, to increase understanding between African Americans and Africa. Robeson was a much-loved international figure, but his sympathy for communism led to his U.S. passport being withdrawn (1950–58).

Before his premature death, Malcolm X, too, built up new international connections and contacts, traveling widely in Africa between 1959 and 1964, after which he established the Organization of African-American Unity (OAAU).

A fascination with African origins, and with the black pride preached by Marcus Garvey, led to the growth of a new religious movement in Jamaica in the 1930s. Its followers believe that Emperor Haile Selassie of Ethiopia (1892–1975) was the symbol of God on Earth, or Jah. Selassie was originally known as Ras Tafari Makonnen, and so believers became known as

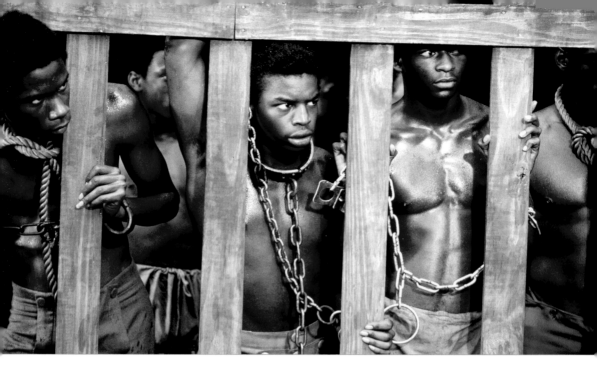

The television version of **Roots** (1977) followed the story of a West African family over the generations. It brought home the reality of the slave trade to a mass audience around the world.

Rastafarians. They called for a return to Africa after centuries of slavery. They gained many followers in the 1960s and 1970s, being associated with the popular reggae music of the day. Rastafarians wear their hair in matted dreadlocks and use the illegal drug marijuana for religious purposes.

In 1966, Pan-African supporters in the U.S.A. invented a new holiday for African Americans to celebrate each year, called Kwanzaa. It is a celebration of African tradition and is marked by feasting, the lighting of candles, and the giving of presents.

One of the most influential books to focus the world's attention on the slave trade and African-American history was a popular novel by the African-American writer, Alex Haley, published in 1976. It was called *Roots: the Saga of an American Family* and was made into a popular television series in 1977.

SPEECH

"We're not Americans, we're Africans who happen to be in America. We were kidnapped and brought here against our will from Africa. We didn't land on Plymouth Rock—that rock landed on us."

Malcolm X emphasizes African origins. Plymouth Rock was where North America's most famous white settlers, the "Pilgrim Fathers," landed in 1620.

Past, present, future…

In 2007, the first phase of a new International Slavery Museum was opened in Liverpool, England, a city that had profited a great deal from slavery in the 1700s. This year marked the 200th anniversary of Britain banning the slave trade, and the day—August 23—was the United Nations' Slavery Remembrance Day. It was also the anniversary of the Haitian slave uprising in 1791 (see pages 16–17). Docked in the port of Liverpool was a replica of the schooner *Amistad*, which made American history in 1839 (see page 25).

Also in August 2007, veteran African-American civil rights activist, Reverend Jesse Jackson, was touring the United Kingdom. He raised the issue of public apologies for past wrongs inflicted by the slaving nations, but his chief topic was the relationship between liberty, justice, and economic opportunity.

After the destruction of New Orleans in the aftermath of Hurricane Katrina in 2005, the U.S. government was criticized for failing to help the mostly black victims.

The remarkable progress made by people of African descent since the days of slavery has been achieved by countless individual examples of heroism, endurance, and vision. The descendants of slaves are now leading politicians, business people, musicians, academics, writers, actors, entertainers, models, and athletes. In 2009, Barack Obama, an American whose father was originally from Kenya, was inaugurated as the 44th President of the United States of America, a remarkable moment in U.S. history.

However, the bigger picture gives pause for reflection. African Americans represent an exceptionally high proportion of prisoners in U.S. jails, the result of the ongoing poverty, deprivation, and poor education prevalent in their communities. Black pupils struggle in schools in the United Kingdom, for similar reasons. Racist political parties seek respectability across Europe. Internet "blogs" spout age-old prejudice and hatred. Despite past successes, there is still a long way to go. Equality cannot be achieved until there is economic justice.

If that is true within the societies of Europe and North America, it is even more so in modern Africa, which is plagued by drought, hunger, and disease. The lack of justice within the global trading system condemns most modern Africans to a life of servitude every bit as much as the transatlantic slave trade did in its day.

Former president Bill Clinton backed Barack Obama in his presidential campaign saying: "[Obama] is ready to lead America."

What often goes unmentioned in the Western press is the spirit of ordinary African people, their inventiveness, hard work, and goodwill. That is the same spirit of endurance that helped them survive the evils of slavery—and it is that which provides hope for the future.

Slavery today

In 1927, an international Slavery Convention was drawn up, supposedly to signal the end of slavery throughout the world. When we study the history of the transatlantic slave trade and its abolition, we often assume that slavery and servitude are things of the past.

In fact, slavery and servitude still affect the lives of about 27 million people worldwide—probably more than at any previous time in history. These evils take many forms, including debt bondage, sexual slavery, child labor, and traditional slavery in which people are treated as personal property. Human trafficking, the forcing of people into servitude,

"Stop the trafficking of children" was the theme of this Day of the African Child rally, in Kenya.

takes place not just in underdeveloped parts of the world, but in the smart and wealthy cities of Europe and North America. It is a multibillion dollar business. Refugees, asylum seekers, and economic migrants also find themselves forced into servitude— unable to return home, unable to find legal work, and treated as criminals instead of victims.

By documenting history, we can learn from the past. Slavery is an evil that still threatens to poison the future of the planet. It can only be eradicated by the vigorous defense of human rights and civil liberties, and by a concept of justice that includes equal economic opportunity for all the world's citizens.

TIMELINE

BCE

ca. 3500	Slavery in Mesopotamia (modern Iraq).
ca. 1000	Slavery in China.

CE

800s	Start of East African slave trade.
1440s	Portuguese transport slaves from Africa to Europe.
1470s	Spain enters the slave trade.
1510	Slave trade on a large scale between Africa and the Americas.
1550	England enters the slave trade.
1776	American Declaration of Independence.
1772	Slavery illegal in England and Wales.
1778	Slavery illegal in Scotland.
1780–1804	Slavery abolished in northern U.S.A.
1787	Britain: Society for Effecting the Abolition of the Slave Trade formed.
	Settlement of freed slaves formed, Sierra Leone.
1788	*La Société des Amis des Noirs* formed, France.
1791–1804	Slave uprising leads to Haitian Revolution.
1794	French revolutionary government decrees emancipation of slaves in the French empire.
1804	Haiti becomes an independent nation under black rule.
1807	Slave Trade Act abolishes slave trade in British empire.
1810–51	The "Underground Railroad" creates escape routes for slaves, U.S.A.
1822	Settlement of freed slaves, Liberia (American Colonization Society).
1833	Death of William Wilberforce; slavery abolished in British empire.
1839	African slaves mutiny on *Amistad*.
1848	Final abolition of slavery in French empire.
1852	*Uncle Tom's Cabin* by Harriet Beecher Stowe is published.
1861–65	American Civil War.
1865	13th Amendment to U.S. Constitution.
1865	Morant Bay Rebellion, Jamaica.
1868	14th Amendment to U.S. Constitution.
1870	15th Amendment to U.S. Constitution.
1873	Zanzibar closes slave market; end of East African trade.
1875	Civil Rights Act, U.S.A.
1888	Brazil abolishes slavery.
1914	Jamaican Marcus Garvey founds the UNIA-ACL in the U.S.A.
1930	Nation of Islam (NoI) formed, U.S.A.
1948	Universal Declaration of Human Rights.
1948–90	South Africa is ruled by an apartheid system.
1955	Murder of Emmett Till, Mississippi.
	Montgomery Bus Boycott, Alabama.
1961	Freedom Riders protest, U.S.A.
1962	Jamaica and Trinidad achieve independence.
1963	Dr. Martin Luther King's address, Washington, DC: "*I have a dream.*"
1965	Voting Rights Act; Murder of Malcolm X: Riots in Watts, Los Angeles.
1965–2001	Race Relations Acts, U.K..
1966	The Black Panther Party founded in the U.S.A.
1968	Dr. Martin Luther King assassinated.
2007	200th anniversary of the abolition of the slave trade, U.K.
2009	Barack Obama inaugurated 44th President of the United States.

GLOSSARY

Abolition movement
Movement to end something.

Affirmative action
The policy of awarding jobs and benefits to an underprivileged class, in order to remedy social injustice.

Apartheid
The policy of strict racial segregation enforced by the government of South Africa from 1948–90.

Apprentice
Someone contracted to work for another during a set period, in order to learn a craft or trade.

Assassinate
To murder someone.

Black Codes
Racist laws enacted in the Southern U.S. states in the nineteenth century.

Black Power
A radical political movement originating in the U.S.A. in the 1960s.

Black pride
A slogan encouraging positive attitudes and assertiveness among black people.

Boycott
To refuse to buy goods or services, or to deal with someone, as a form of protest.

Brand
To burn a mark of ownership on to the skin of a slave or the hide of cattle, using a red-hot iron.

Cash crop
A crop grown for sale and profit rather than for subsistence.

Civil rights
The basic rights that every human being deserves within society, such as a vote or freedom of speech.

Colony
A territory that is ruled or settled by another country.

Communism
Radical socialism that supports a state-controlled or state-directed economy. Political movement that represents the working class.

Debt bondage
Being forced to work for someone else until a debt is repaid.

Discrimination
To make a distinction, for instance, by favoring one social group above another.

Economic migrant
Someone who leaves their home country for economic reasons, to seek work elsewhere.

Emancipation
Freeing, releasing, liberating.

Federal
Relating to a form of government in which power is divided between one central and several regional governments.

Fettered
Bound by iron chains or bars.

Founding fathers
The men who founded the United States of America and who drafted and agreed its Constitution.

Ghetto
An area of a city in which an ethnic group is isolated, politically or economically.

Human rights
The basic conditions of liberty, justice, and equality that all human beings deserve.

Imperialism
The politics and economics associated with ruling empires and colonies.

Indenture
A contract of employment over a long term, during which the employee forfeits the right to move away or withdraw labor.

Indigenous
Native, belonging to an area.

Legislature
A body, such as a parliament, that has the authority to pass or review laws.

Lynching
The public killing of a suspected criminal or scapegoat by a mob.

Manumission
A legal release from slavery; being set free.

Maroons
Slaves who escaped to form independent communities in remote parts of South America and the Caribbean.

Middle Passage
The voyage of slave ships from Africa to the New World, the second stage of the Triangular Trade.

Minstrel shows
Song and dance shows in which white performers dressed as black people and sang in an affected "Negro" style.

Nationalist
Seeking independence as a nation.

Nonviolent direct action
Protesting forcefully but avoiding violent confrontation.

Overseer
A person appointed by the "owner" to supervise slave labor.

Pan-Africanism
A policy of encouraging political and cultural links between Africans and people of African descent from other parts of the world.

Reconstruction
The period of reform in the former Confederate states after the American Civil War.

Refugee
Someone who flees from one country to another to escape war, persecution, or natural disaster.

Scriptures
Writings believed to be sacred within a religion.

Segregation
The enforced social separation of two groups of people, such as blacks and whites.

Serfdom
An economic system in which someone is forced to work in the service of a lord or landowner, and may not move away.

FURTHER INFORMATION AND WEB SITES

FURTHER READING

African American History: Slavery by James (De Medeiros, Weigl Publishers, 2008)

Africans in America: America's Journey Through Slavery by Charles Johnson (Harvest Books, 1999)

American Voices From the Time of Slavery by Elizabeth Sirimarco (Benchmark Books, 2006)

The Interesting Narrative of the Life of Olaudah Equiano by Olaudah Equiano, (Coffeetown Press, 2008)

WEB SITES

Due to the changing nature of Internet links, Rosen Publishing has developed an online list of Web Sites related to the subject of this book. This site is regularly updated. Please use this link to access this list:
http://www.rosenlinks.com/doc/slav

INDEX

Numbers in **bold** refer to illustrations.